STUDY GUIDE

Only Two Religions

Peter Jones

LIGONIER MINISTRIES
Renew your Mind.
LIGONIER.ORG | 800-435-4343

421 Ligonier Court, Sanford, FL 32771
E-mail: info@ligonier.org

Introduction

If you survey the religious landscape of modern culture, you will encounter an astonishingly diverse range of views. But beneath the surface, these seemingly disparate spiritualities share a common worldview, one that is radically opposed to the Christian faith. In this series, join Dr. Peter Jones as he examines the worldview and fundamental religious convictions that drive modern culture. He demonstrates that in the final analysis, there can be only two religions—worship of the Creator or worship of creation. By better understanding the present cultural context, you will be equipped to more clearly articulate the Christian faith and worldview to a world in need of redemption.

1

Explaining Modern Culture

MESSAGE INTRODUCTION

During the 1960s, the United States underwent a paradigm shift in religion. A once-dominant Christian worldview was supplanted by a New Age spirituality that was anything but new. It was, rather, a rearticulation of ancient paganism. This pagan belief system is not limited to certain late-twentieth-century religions; it is the fundamental belief system of all non-Christian religions. One can thus draw a sharp distinction between Christianity, which worships the Creator, and paganism, which worships the creation. In this lecture, Dr. Peter Jones shows that there are only two possible religions. By better understanding other religions that share a common foundation, you will be better equipped to share the gospel with clarity and love.

SCRIPTURE READINGS

Romans 1:18–25; Isaiah 44:9–20

TEACHING OBJECTIVES

1. To introduce the idea that modern culture is the battlefield between only two religions
2. To demonstrate how non-Christian religions share a similar ideology
3. To show the uniqueness of the Christian faith and worldview

QUOTATION

In the light of Scripture we learn to understand that religion is a relation in which man stands to God, a relation in which man is conscious of the absolute majesty and infinite power of God and of his own utter insignificance and absolute helplessness. It may be defined as a conscious and voluntary relationship to God, which expresses itself in grateful worship and loving service. The manner of this religious worship and service is not left to the arbitrary will of man, but is determined by God.

—Louis Berkhof

LECTURE OUTLINE

1. There are ultimately only two religions.
   a. Modern culture is the battleground between these religions.
   b. By understanding both religions, one can understand modern culture.

2. In the West, one religion dominated before the 1960s, another after the 1960s.
   a. Before the 1960s
      i. While not everyone was a Christian, most had a worldview heavily influenced by the biblical tradition.
      ii. This affected their views on theology, morality, sexuality, marriage, etc.
   b. During the 1960s
      i. There was a "cataclysmic change" rather than a normal passing on of traditions from one generation to the next.
      ii. The beliefs that dominated the West were redefined beyond recognition.
   c. After the 1960s
      i. There has been an increasing reassertion of ancient paganism, which was presented as something new.
      ii. This has led to a departure from traditional views of God, morality, sexuality, marriage, etc.

3. The biblical reason for asserting only two religions
   a. In Romans 1:25, Paul identifies two kinds of truth.
      i. One can worship the Creator.
      ii. One can worship the creation.
   b. This provides a paradigm to understand the great variety of religions.

4. The essential beliefs of both religions
   a. Oneism
      i. It is the same as paganism and Gnosticism.
      ii. It is the worship of creation, where everything is one, sharing the same substance.
      iii. It reduces God to a piece of creation, making him the spirit within things.
   b. Twoism
      i. It asserts a clear distinction between Creator and creation.
      ii. The only consistently twoist religion is Christianity.

5. The usefulness of a two-religion analysis of modern culture
   a. Helps to identify and understand what's happening in modern culture.
   b. Helps to see how modern culture has influenced the church.
   c. It shows that all non-Christian religions share a similar aim to reduce two to one, to destroy the distinction between Creator and creation.
      i. Progressive spirituality
         1. It is the name for modern spirituality.

        2. The goal of thinking is non-dual consciousness.
        3. Non-dual is good, and any duality is bad.
    ii. Hinduism
        1. It is argued that a Hindu ideology in which all is one is taking over America.
        2. The important Sanskrit word for this is *Advaita*, "not two."
    iii. Islam
        1. Sufism (a branch of Islam) argues that Allah is everything and we are everything, too, which is oneism.
        2. Orthodox Islam
            a. For Allah to be personal he had to create.
            b. If he had to create, then he's dependent.
            c. The Creator's dependence on creation is oneism.
  d. It demonstrates the truthfulness and the essential coherence of the Christian faith.
    i. Only the triune God can be separate from creation.
    ii. Only the triune God is personal in His very essence.

6. Modern culture will adopt one of the two religions.
    a. It can reform and embrace the Christian, twoist religion.
    b. It can further embrace a pagan, oneist religion, and thus redefine Western civilization on the lie that nature is God.

7. Christians must faithfully respond to the increasing dominance of pagan thought.
    a. They must identify the ideology at the root of the various modern spiritualities.
    b. They must articulate the gospel message.

STUDY QUESTIONS

1. *Advaita* is a Sanskrit term meaning ________.
    a. All is one
    b. All is god
    c. Not one
    d. Not two

2. Islam is a religion that exemplifies consistent twoism.
    a. True
    b. False

3. Which of the following terms is synonymous with oneism?
    a. Paganism
    b. Atheism
    c. Pantheism
    d. Gnosticism

4. The only ultimate choice in religion is whether one will worship the Creator or the creation.
   a. True
   b. False

5. The change in Western religion that occurred in the 1960s has been characterized as a ________.
   a. Gradual shift
   b. Religious revival
   c. Reformation
   d. Cataclysmic transformation

BIBLE STUDY AND DISCUSSION QUESTIONS

1. What are some ways that oneism manifests itself in popular television shows, movies, or books?

2. Within your own lifetime, have you seen your culture move further away from a Christian worldview? What are some areas in which you've witnessed this?

3. What are some motivations for Christians to take the time to study other religions?

4. Is the political arena an appropriate place for Christians to try to influence a country with their worldview? Why or why not?

2

The Rise and Fall of Secular Humanism

MESSAGE INTRODUCTION

We live in a society that has seen tremendous development in science and technology. This development has been intimately tied to an ideology called secular humanism, which views human reason as the ultimate authority and rejects the supernatural. Modern culture, however, is very open to the supernatural and countless forms of spirituality. In this lecture, Dr. Peter Jones explains the development of secular humanism, tracing its origin, rise to dominance, and eventual decline. By understanding this influential ideological movement, you will be better prepared to understand the modern culture in which you live.

SCRIPTURE READINGS

Psalm 53; 2 Corinthians 10:1–5

TEACHING OBJECTIVES

1. To explain the history of secular humanism and its influence on modern culture
2. To expose how secular humanism has affected the church in the form of theological liberalism
3. To show why secular humanism has failed to provide an alternative religion to Christianity

QUOTATION

The expression of David (Psalm 14:1, 53:1), "The fool hath said in his heart, There is no God," is primarily applied to those who . . . stifle the light of nature, and intentionally stupefy themselves. We see many, after they have become hardened in a daring course of sin, madly banishing all remembrance of God, though spontaneously suggested to them from within, by natural sense. To show how detestable this madness is, the Psalmist

> *introduces them as distinctly denying that there is a God, because although they do not disown his essence, they rob him of his justice and providence, and represent him as sitting idly in heaven. Nothing being less accordant with the nature of God than to cast off the government of the world, leaving it to chance, and so to wink at the crimes of men that they may wanton with impunity in evil courses; it follows, that every man who indulges in security, after extinguishing all fear of divine Judgment, virtually denies that there is a God. As a just punishment of the wicked, after they have closed their own eyes, God makes their hearts dull and heavy, and hence, seeing, they see not.*
>
> —John Calvin

LECTURE OUTLINE

1. There are two non-Christian ideologies that powerfully influence modern culture.
   a. Secular humanism: the focus of this lecture
   b. Paganism: the focus of future lectures
   c. It will be shown that both of these ideologies are oneist.

2. Humanism gained influence during the Renaissance.
   a. Humanism celebrated the value of the human individual and his reason over against the power of the church.
   b. Human reason went from being valued to becoming the only source of truth.

3. Humanism gained dominance after the Enlightenment.
   a. Humanism was characterized by optimism for what mankind could achieve.
      i. This thinking dominated in universities.
      ii. It proclaimed a oneist view that depended on humans to put the world together.
   b. It was vividly expressed in the French Revolution.
   c. Leading intellectuals of the eighteenth and nineteenth centuries predicted the end of religion.

4. Secular humanism has greatly influenced modern views of religion.
   a. Intellectuals called Christianity "a delusion," "a gigantic human projection," "the opiate of the people," and "a kind of mental illness," and proclaimed the "death of God."
   b. Leading philosophers argued that they were not religious, but rather rational.
   c. It has influenced a rationalistic approach to religion whereby faith is seen as a form of illness.

5. Secular humanism has affected the church.
   a. This is characteristic of liberalism—the adaptation of the world's thinking and trying to make it Christian.
   b. The gospel was redefined as social work or Marxist politics, and Jesus was seen as an example rather than a divine savior.

6. Darwin's theory of natural selection further supported secular humanism.
    a. Darwin's work effectively replaced God as the Creator with the idea of an unguided, impersonal process of natural selection.
    b. According to this view, everything is the result of purposeless chance.
    c. Science came to be seen as the only way to know anything.

7. Secular humanism was thought to have triumphed over Christianity.
    a. There was a decline of the Christian faith in America.
    b. In the 1970s, some proclaimed the death of God and the victory of secular humanism.

8. There are intellectual, religious, and political forms of secular humanism.
    a. Intellectual: philosophical materialism, which argues that matter is ultimate; there is no supernatural
    b. Religious: atheism, the belief that there is no god
    c. Political: Marxism and forms of socialism
    d. For many, secular humanism is the default way of thinking and living.

9. Secular humanism has and continues to decline.
    a. While on the decline, secular humanism still dominates Western universities.
    b. Rather than seeing the predicted withering away of religion, we are seeing a withering away of secular humanism.
        i. Many now claim to be spiritual but not religious, and being spiritual doesn't fit with secular humanism.
        ii. The optimism of secular humanism has been diminished by two world wars, industrialization, and ecological disasters.
        iii. Many people feel that they cannot exist in this world without some form of spirituality, which secular humanism does not provide.
    c. Secular humanism is a weak system philosophically.
        i. It is inherently circular.
        ii. To demonstrate the validity of human reason, one must presuppose it, but presupposing it is really a statement of faith that the world is rational.
    d. There are two primary reasons for the decline of secular humanism.
        i. It cannot stand against biblical theism.
        ii. It is being supplanted by a new spirituality.

STUDY QUESTIONS

1. During the French Revolution, the Paris revolutionaries built an altar to ________.
    a. The Lord
    b. A bull
    c. Reason
    d. Zeus

2. *Demythologizing* means taking away the myths and getting to the heart, which is a sense of one's own self being faced with nothingness.
   a. True
   b. False

3. The political form of secular humanism is ________.
   a. Philosophical materialism
   b. Atheism
   c. Marxism
   d. Paganism

4. Secular humanism continues to dominate Western universities.
   a. True
   b. False

5. ________ is responsible for the phrase *écrasez l'infâme*, which means "crush the infamous," and became the battle cry of the French Revolution.
   a. Montesquieu
   b. Voltaire
   c. Dumas
   d. Diderot

BIBLE STUDY AND DISCUSSION QUESTIONS

1. Dr. Jones argues that as Western culture has made great advances through science and technology, it has become more enamored with the power and ability of human reason. Can you think of episodes in Scripture where success leads to pride? Do you think that there is a direct relationship between a society's success and its morality?

2. Read Mark 4:26–34. Compare the secular humanist view of bringing about the kingdom of man on earth with Christ's description of the growth of the kingdom of God. What are the primary differences between their respective modes of arrival?

3. Despite the cry of numerous intellectuals over the past few centuries, religion shows no sign of going away. When Christians in particular have their faith belittled by such intellectuals, how should they respond? What is their ultimate comfort amid this type of adversity?

4. What sort of evidence do you see in modern culture that suggests the waning influence of secular humanism? In what areas of culture do people still cling to a secular humanist ideology?

3

Carl Jung's Alternative Spirituality

MESSAGE INTRODUCTION

In the last lecture, we saw the growth and decline of secular humanism. This ideology had a powerful effect on religion in the West, but the spiritual void that it left was quickly filled by a new spirituality. In this lecture, Dr. Jones demonstrates that Carl Jung, the Swiss psychologist, was essential in the development of this so-called new spirituality. He espoused a pagan ideology that emphasized the joining of opposites, and thus relativized right and wrong, male and female, and other relationships.

SCRIPTURE READINGS

Isaiah 5:20–21; Luke 11:34–35

TEACHING OBJECTIVES

1. To explain the ideas espoused by the Swiss psychologist Carl Jung
2. To explain Jung's great influence on modern culture
3. To understand how Jung was able to have so much influence

QUOTATION

That there exists in the human minds and indeed by natural instinct, some sense of Deity, we hold to be beyond dispute, since God himself, to prevent any man from pretending ignorance, has endued all men with some idea of his Godhead, the memory of which he constantly renews and occasionally enlarges, that all to a man being aware that there is a God, and that he is their Maker, may be condemned by their own conscience when they neither worship him nor consecrate their lives to his service.

—John Calvin

LECTURE OUTLINE

1. David Miller, a follower of Carl Jung, predicted that there would be a rejection of the Christian God and a return to polytheism.

2. Carl Jung (1875–1961) was essential in the production of modern culture.
   a. He was a Swiss clinical psychologist.
   b. Jung conspired with his colleague Mircea Eliade, an expert in pagan religions, to envision what they called a new humanism.

3. Jung was driven by the idea that myth is the search to understand the self.
   a. Our fantasies actually give expression to the gods of pagan myths throughout history.
   b. This is the direction and source of psychological health.

4. Jung advocated a system called transpersonal psychology.
   a. It was based on two things.
      i. Jung's experience of the occult
      ii. Pagan traditions that had recently been made available
   b. It stated that the subconscious is guided by the pagan ideal of the joining of the opposites.
   c. A person gets in touch with his inner subconscious by joining together the inner contradictions within himself and meditating on the pagan archetypes, which are the understandings of spirituality found in pagan religions.
   d. The ultimate goal of transpersonal psychology is *individuation*, the removal of contradictions within a person.
   e. This joining of opposites heals guilt, eliminates notions of divine transcendence, and breaks the chain of heterosexual monogamous marriage.

5. Jung rejected Christ and chose the gnostic god Abraxas.
   a. Abraxas is half-man, half-beast.
   b. He is considered higher than the Christian God and the devil, combining everything.
   c. While practicing the emptying of his consciousness to see what was beneath, Jung talks about a pagan spirit guide named Philemon who took him to Abraxas.

6. Carl Jung and Mircea Eliade saw themselves as architects of a new humanism that would deliver the world from two blights.
   a. Secular humanism
      i. They wanted to see intellectuals who were influenced by secular humanism open their minds to the spiritual world.
      ii. They accomplished this by using scientific language when talking about spiritual things.
   b. Traditional Christianity

7. Jung had specific goals, and he devised means to reach those goals.
    a. "The new religion and its proclamation, a new ordering of human affairs."
    b. He wanted everyone to beware of thinking of good and evil as absolute opposites.
    c. He wanted to produce a unitary world.
    d. He wanted to liberate sexuality, saying that its liberation was key for psychological and spiritual health.
    e. He produced a therapeutic mechanism for the individual subconscious to be liberated from the mental illness of guilt by joining or relativizing the opposites of right and wrong, male and female, etc.
        i. Jung succeeded in this technique by getting people to believe that what their unconscious fantasy tells them is true.
        ii. We're building a world on that basis.

8. Jung used different language with different audiences to make his ideas acceptable.
    a. Scientific language with intellectuals
    b. Spiritual language with his inner circle

9. Jung recognized that there was a need for a spirituality for a culture losing its faith in secular humanism.

10. Biographer Richard Noll argued that Jung succeeded where the apostate Roman Emperor Julian had failed.
    a. He helped undermine orthodox Christianity.
    b. He turned people toward pagan polytheism.

STUDY QUESTIONS

1. Jung called the removal of contradictions within the individual ________.
    a. Self-realization
    b. Individuation
    c. Liberation
    d. Ultimate conflation
2. In order to make his ideas more acceptable to intellectuals, Carl Jung described his ideas using modern scientific language.
    a. True
    b. False
3. Jung rejected the Christian God and embraced the gnostic god ________, who was half-man, half-beast, and combined God and the devil.
    a. Abraxas
    b. Pleroma
    c. Sophia
    d. The demiurge

4. Jung and Eliade sought to deliver the world from secular humanism and traditional Christianity.
   a. True
   b. False
5. Jung's system that was designed to bring everyone to a higher level of personal liberation was called ________.
   a. Actualization
   b. Transcendental meditation
   c. Transpersonal psychology
   d. Psychotherapy

BIBLE STUDY AND DISCUSSION QUESTIONS

1. How should Christians respond to oneist ideologies that seek to eliminate distinctions?

2. How does the joining of opposites relieve guilt that a person feels? Contrast this approach with the Christian understanding of where guilt comes from and how it should be addressed.

3. Jung had as a goal the liberation of sexuality for psychological and spiritual health. Many today would accuse Christians of repressing their sexuality, arguing that doing so leads to harmful results. How should Christians respond to such accusations?

4. Jung said that we must beware of thinking of good and evil as absolute opposites. What would this do for morality?

4

Paganism in the Shadows

MESSAGE INTRODUCTION

The multitude of religions that we encounter in modern culture may seem novel, but they are simply the latest manifestations of the ancient pagan traditions that have been known throughout human history. In this lecture, Dr. Jones surveys numerous religions, ancient and modern, and demonstrates that they share the same essential commitments.

SCRIPTURE READINGS

Ecclesiastes 1:9–10; Colossians 2:16–23

TEACHING OBJECTIVES

1. To survey various expressions of paganism, ancient and modern
2. To show that what Carl Jung offered was not something new, but rather a repackaging of ancient paganism
3. To demonstrate that despite the many variations of pagan religion, they share the same essential commitments

QUOTATION

The Bible gives the only reliable account of the origin of religion. It informs us of the existence of God, the only object worthy of religious worship. Moreover, it comes to us with the assurance that God, whom man could never discover with his natural powers, revealed Himself in nature and, more especially, in His divine Word, demands the worship and service of man, and also determines the worship and service that is well-pleasing to Him. And, finally, it teaches us that God created man in His own image, and thus endowed him with a capacity to understand, and to respond to, this revelation, and engendered in him a natural urge to seek communion with God and to glorify Him.

—Louis Berkhof

LECTURE OUTLINE

1. Carl Jung was and was not an innovator.
   a. He *was* an innovator because he tied growing interest in pagan spirituality to new psychological methodology.
   b. He *was not* an innovator because the paganism he proposed was ancient.

2. What was once secret and esoteric is now being seen clearly.

3. Paganism was driven underground by the early triumph of Christianity.

4. The hundreds of variations of pagan religion share the same essential commitments.
   a. Second-century Gnostics taught the great mystery of God within.
      i. They called their religion "the true religion that should be veiled in deep silence."
      ii. They believed that all religions are co-witnesses to the secret principle—the omnipresence of the divine principle and the power of gnosis.
   b. The Freemasons
      i. They call their religion the "Sacred Secret" or the "Ageless Wisdom."
      ii. It was defined as "the religion in which all men agree."
   c. The Theosophical Society claims to espouse the "secret teaching of all the ages."
   d. The Wiccans
      i. Speak of "old wisdom" that is encapsulated in the phrase "as above, so below."
      ii. They seek the joining of opposites into one.
      iii. Their ideology is founded in ancient Gnosticism.
      iv. The book *The Secret* holds this same ideology.
   e. The "Great Work"
      i. In medieval alchemy, the great work was to join the human and divine.
      ii. Thomas Berry argued that the great work in modern times is to reinvent the human at the species level by means of shared dream experiences.

STUDY QUESTIONS

1. Since there is such a great variety of non-Christian religions, it cannot accurately be said that they share fundamental commitments.
   a. True
   b. False

2. The phrase that encapsulates Wiccan ideology is ________.
   a. Old wisdom
   b. The great work
   c. As above, so below
   d. The joining of opposites

3. The Perennial Philosophy is the fundamental notion that nature is divine.
   a. True
   b. False

4. The great work of medieval alchemy was to join ________ and ________.
   a. The divine, nature
   b. The divine, the human
   c. Good, evil
   d. Light, darkness

5. Gnosis means ________.
   a. Unity
   b. Knowledge
   c. Not two
   d. Vision

BIBLE STUDY AND DISCUSSION QUESTIONS

1. How can the claim that non-Christian religions share fundamental beliefs com fort Christians who are confused at the bewildering diversity of religions in modern culture?

2. Thomas Berry believes that our contemporary calling is to carry on the great work of the American Indians, following their traditions and spirituality. Have you seen this pushed in the portrayal of American Indians in modern culture, whether through film or publications?

3. Have you ever interacted with a practitioner of Wicca or another modern spirituality?

4. Prince Charles said that the sacralization of nature is what will solve the environmental crisis of the twenty-first century. Critique this statement from a twoist perspective.

5

Paganism in the Spotlight

MESSAGE INTRODUCTION

The 1960s saw what some have called a pagan revival, and what others have described as a cataclysmic change. It was a period in which the influence of Christianity waned and alternative spiritualities filled the void. Many modern spiritual movements began during this time, and embodied the pagan ideology of Carl Jung. By examining the history and influence of these religions, one can better grasp their similarities and understand how they have had such an influence on modern culture.

SCRIPTURE READINGS

Romans 3:10–18; Psalm 14

TEACHING OBJECTIVES

1. To show that the spiritual movement of the 1960s was a pagan revival
2. To show the drastic change in spirituality during the 1960s
3. To demonstrate how what was marginal in the 1960s has become mainstream in the present

QUOTATION

The present religious confusion of those who would base their religion on a purely natural basis clearly proves its insufficiency. It does not even afford an adequate basis for religion in general, much less for true religion. Even gentile nations appeal to some supposed special revelation. And, finally, it utterly fails to meet the spiritual needs of sinners. While it conveys some knowledge of the goodness, the wisdom, and the power of God, it conveys no knowledge whatever of Christ as the only way of salvation.

—Louis Berkhof

LECTURE OUTLINE

1. The spirituality under discussion represents a sort of hidden esoteric tradition.
   a. It comes to the surface openly in the 1960s.
   b. It represents the fulfillment of Jung's vision of a society liberated to practice pagan spirituality.

2. The 1960s saw a pagan revival.
   a. Described as a serendipitous confluence of events
      i. Decline of Christianity
      ii. Growth of alternative spiritualities
   b. Many modern spiritual movements began in the 1960s.
      i. They distance themselves from secular humanism.
      ii. They eliminate the notion of religion, especially Christianity.

3. It is now argued that there is only one faith that speaks in many tongues.
   a. Christians are pressured to acknowledge this.
   b. Those who deny this new tenet run the risk of being cast as those who are not open to the future.

4. The marginal 1960s spirituality has become mainstream.
   a. It's encapsulated in the phrase "I'm spiritual but not religious."
   b. Jung's idea that the divine reigns within and that fantasies are morally justified
      i. This brings psychological health.
      ii. It brings completion of ourselves and the health of the planet.

5. The pagan vision of the world is being applied to all of existence—science, law, education, politics, sexuality, ecology, and ethics.
   a. It seeks to discover the divine as a dimension of the human.
   b. It is a fulfillment of what Jung was looking for—a new humanity.

6. The new spirituality does not allow private religion.
   a. It imposes its new vision of existence upon everyone.
   b. It seeks to be the dominant worldview.

7. Many claim that America has become Hindu.
   a. Many Americans espouse a Hindu worldview.
   b. Yoga is being taught in schools.
   c. The oneist ideology that everything is one eliminates a God who is separate.

8. Reasons for the turn to Eastern religions
   a. Carl Jung
   b. Parliament on the World's Religions

9. There is a shift in the West in which the center of spiritual gravity is moving away from Judeo-Christian theology and to the occult.

STUDY QUESTIONS

1. The pagan vision of the world is now being applied to all areas—science, law, education, politics, sexuality, ecology, and ethics.
   a. True
   b. False
2. Some have called the present-day spiritual movement ________.
   a. The Fourth Great Awakening
   b. A new reformation
   c. The age of light
   d. The liberation of the spirit
3. The new spirituality is content to let everyone practice their own religion.
   a. True
   b. False
4. A characteristic phrase of the new spirituality is ________.
   a. "Live and let live"
   b. "We're spiritual but not religious"
   c. "Judge not"
   d. "To each his own"
5. The Age of Aquarius refers to the moment in the zodiacal system where the Age of Pisces, represented by a fish, is superseded by the age of the goddess who brings spiritual drink.
   a. True
   b. False

BIBLE STUDY AND DISCUSSION QUESTIONS

1. One of the characteristics of the new spirituality is that people claim to practice spirituality without being religious. Have you seen a parallel in the church? What are the dangers of this sort of thinking?

2. Have you participated in or witnessed an interfaith movement? Do you think such movements help or hurt the spread of the Christian faith and worldview?

3. Many in today's society want to see Christianity conform to the idea that all forms of religion are equally valid expressions. How should Christians combat this view?

4. How can Christians demonstrate that their refusal to conform is actually an expression of love for others?

6

Pagan Sexuality

MESSAGE INTRODUCTION

Together with the radical spiritual changes that took place in the 1960s, there was a sexual revolution. Christian notions of sexuality were jettisoned in favor of pagan ideals that sought to eliminate gender distinctions and any idea of right or wrong with regard to sexuality. In this lecture, you will see the origin, nature, and character of this sexual revolution, and you will better understand why it has and continues to be such a powerful force in modern culture.

SCRIPTURE READINGS

Romans 1:26–27; Genesis 2:18–25

TEACHING OBJECTIVES

1. To explain the liberation of sexuality that occurred during the twentieth century
2. To show how sexual liberation has been promoted by the most influential in society
3. To demonstrate the radical contrast between pagan oneist and Christian twoist views of sexuality

QUOTATION

But though experience testifies that a seed of religion is divinely sown in all, scarcely one in a hundred is found who cherishes it in his heart, and not one in whom it grows to maturity so far is it from yielding fruit in its season. Moreover, while some lose themselves in superstitious observances, and others, of set purpose, wickedly revolt from God, the result is that, in regard to the true knowledge of him, all are so degenerate, that in no part of the world can genuine godliness be found.

—John Calvin

LECTURE OUTLINE

1. The 1960s saw a liberation of sexuality in addition to a liberation of spirituality.
   a. This is a fulfillment of Jung's ideas.
   b. Jung had promoted sexual freedom as the path to psychological wholeness and health.
   c. Christian notions of restraint were characterized as repressive and harmful to one's health.

2. Those who took part in the cultural takeover of the 1960s became influential in society and promoted sexual liberation.
   a. They run the nation's most prestigious universities.
   b. They run broadcast networks, newspapers, legal firms, Hollywood, and the U.S. government.
   c. They run education, which teaches the "values" of sexual liberation to children.
   d. The liberating view of sexuality is being systematically promoted in modern culture.

3. The extent of sexual liberation is seen in queer theory.
   a. Queer theory rejects the idea that sexuality is determined by biology or eternal standards of truth.
   b. One's fantasy determines reality.
   c. Queer theory continues and even goes beyond Jung's promotion of sexual fulfilment.

4. The effect of sexual liberation is seen in the millennial generation.
   a. They acknowledge no inherently male/female roles.
   b. The future goal is to get rid of the entire notion of gender.

5. The homosexuality and androgyny that is promoted is in line with ancient paganism.
   a. Androgyny has long been seen as a valid expression of wholeness in paganism.
   b. Leaders of pagan cults have often been homosexual shamans.

6. Androgyny is seen as a sacrament.
   a. It is a symbol carrying spiritual meaning.
   b. It symbolizes primordial cosmic unity—everything is one.

7. The sexual perversion that is prevalent in society is a direct result of humanity worshiping the creation rather than the Creator.

STUDY QUESTIONS

1. The next step in the liberation of sexuality is to establish the dominance of the female sex.
   a. True
   b. False
2. Jung's followers argued that Christian notions of sexual constraint were ________.
   a. Examples of moral fortitude
   b. Harmful to one's psychological health
   c. Adopted from ancient pagan ideals
   d. Models to be emulated
3. Queer theory insists that the most fulfilling relationships are homosexual in nature.
   a. True
   b. False
4. Mircea Eliade showed that throughout time and space, leaders of pagan cults are often ________.
   a. Women
   b. Medicine men
   c. Homosexual shamans
   d. Ecstatic visionaries
5. Jung believed that doing evil could have a beneficial effect on the personality by freeing the psyche from one-sidedness and putting one back in touch with one's instinctual being.
   a. True
   b. False

BIBLE STUDY AND DISCUSSION QUESTIONS

1. Many today claim that Christian ideas of sexual restraint are psychologically damaging. How can Christians respond to such claims? How can they challenge those who have opposing opinions on sexuality?

2. Dr. Jones argues that pagan notions of sexuality have been promoted in many sectors of modern culture. Where have you seen this to be especially the case? What is an appropriate Christian response?

3. How does the pagan view of sexuality relate to the pagan view of all reality?

4. Explain the modern push for same-sex marriage in light of the material from this lecture.

7

From Personal Spirituality to Worldview

MESSAGE INTRODUCTION

The New Age movement focused on the individual's spirituality, but over time certain individuals sought to develop their experiences into a worldview for everyone. This worldview rejects both Christianity and atheism, but rather than presenting a novel alternative, it merely rearticulates the ancient pagan worldview. This lecture will show how this worldview developed and its basis.

SCRIPTURE READINGS

Acts 17:22–34; John 14:6

TEACHING OBJECTIVES

1. To show how the new spirituality has gone from a focus on the self to the development of a worldview
2. To explain the character of the post-secular, post-Christian worldview
3. To demonstrate that the new worldview is really a rearticulation of the pagan worldview

QUOTATION

Here it is that natural theology utterly fails. It cannot answer the question, How can man be just with God? or, How can God be just and yet justify the ungodly? Mankind have anxiously pondered this question for ages, and have gained no satisfaction. The ear has been placed on the bosom of humanity, to catch the still, small voice of conscience, and got no answer. It has been directed heavenward, and received no response. Reason, conscience, tradition, history, unite in saying that sin is death; and, therefore, that so far as human wisdom and resources are concerned, the salvation of sinners is as impossible as raising the dead. Every conceivable method of expiation and purification has been tried without success.

—Charles Hodge

LECTURE OUTLINE

1. Spiritual progressives are trying to develop a comprehensive pagan worldview.
    a. It is no longer focused on the individual self.
    b. Powerful people want to turn their individual experience into a worldview for everyone.

2. We are seeing a new spirituality that consists of Native American spirituality plus Eastern mysticism.
    a. It gets rid of any notion of God as an external authority.
    b. This vision is being introduced into many college campuses via the notion of sustainability.
    c. Radical sexual notions are included in ideas of sustainability.

3. World purificationism is a nonreligious apocalyptic movement that preaches global human renewal and predicts apocalypse as the alternative.

4. Post-secularism
    a. Rejection of Christianity
    b. Rejection of atheism

5. Four pillars supporting the post-secular view
    a. New psychology
        i. Jung is taken as the model of the intellectual scientist able to penetrate into the mysteries of the spiritual.
        ii. Defense of the occult by intellectual scientific inquiry
    b. New science
    c. Recovered nature spirituality
    d. Modern feminism

STUDY QUESTIONS

1. Post-secularism rejects *both* Christianity and atheism.
    a. True
    b. False

2. Dr. Jones believes that the two most important factors that motivate human beings are ________ and ________.
    a. Spirituality, psychology
    b. Spirituality, sexuality
    c. Sexuality, culture
    d. Spirituality, culture

3. A major pillar of the post-secular worldview is the recovery of nature spirituality.
   a. True
   b. False

4. The descendants of the New Age movement now refer to themselves as all of the following except ________.
   a. Cultural creatives
   b. Brights
   c. Integral spiritualists
   d. Global visionaries

5. The philosopher Richard Tarnas believes that the human story is culminating in a great synthesis bringing together the two tendencies of Western history—the autonomous mind of the scientist and the wild spirit of the romantics.
   a. True
   b. False

BIBLE STUDY AND DISCUSSION QUESTIONS

1. Dr. Jones noted that the ancient Babylonians made pagan religion fashionable by incorporating art, drama, and music into their religion. Can you think of some instances of this occurring in the United States?

2. The idea that humanity can unite to save the planet has become very popular in recent years. What is the problem with this idea? What alternative can Christians offer?

3. How does the shift of focus from an individual's spirituality to the construction of a worldview result in a more active promotion of paganism?

4. Compare and contrast the Christian hope for the future with that of the so-called world purificationists, who preach global human renewal and predict apocalypse as its woeful alternative.

8

Where Is Society Headed?

MESSAGE INTRODUCTION

With society's acceptance and adoption of a pagan worldview, one may ask where society is headed. It is becoming increasingly hostile to the Christian worldview, which clearly distinguishes between Creator and creation. It seeks to eliminate this distinction in all areas of life and culture. In this lecture, we will see where society may be heading if it continues to worship the creation rather than the Creator.

SCRIPTURE READINGS

Matthew 7:13–14; Romans 1:32

TEACHING OBJECTIVES

1. To explore the direction society may be headed as a result of its adoption and promotion of oneism
2. To show the manner in which oneist thinking is being promulgated today
3. To contrast the oneist worldview with the Christian worldview

QUOTATION

For the world labors as much as it can to shake off all knowledge of God, and corrupts his worship in innumerable ways. I only say, that, when the stupid hardness of heart, which the wicked eagerly court as a means of despising God, becomes enfeebled, the sense of Deity, which of all things they wished most to be extinguished, is still in vigor, and now and then breaks forth. Whence we infer, that this is not a doctrine which is first learned at school, but one as to which every man is, from the womb, his own master; one which nature herself allows no individual to forget, though many, with all their might, strive to do so. Moreover, if all are born and live for the express purpose of learning to know God, and if the knowledge of God, in so far as it fails to produce this effect, is fleeting and vain, it is clear that all those who do not direct the whole thoughts and actions of their lives to this end fail to fulfil the law of their being.

—John Calvin

LECTURE OUTLINE

1. Where is modern culture heading?
    a. Falling apart
        i. What one scholar considers the principles of cultural success are crumbling—honesty, industry, marriage, and religion.
        ii. A society without virtue cannot stand.
        iii. There is a desire to redefine human civilization based on the idea that man is god.
        iv. There is a rejection of the notion that man is made in God's image.
        v. Promotion of gay rights and queer theory at highest levels
            1. Attempt to overturn the idea that marriage is heterosexual, monogamous
            2. Not only toleration is demanded, but silence from any would-be opponents.
            3. This is being taught in schools.
    b. The denial of boundaries is a hallmark of paganism.
        i. The goal is the joining of opposites.
        ii. Relativizing all notions of morality leads to an immoral culture that is hostile and discriminatory.

2. The elimination of the binary
    a. Epistemology—distinction between true and false abandoned
    b. Science
        i. Humans celebrated as co-creators of the cosmos
        ii. Binary distinction of Creator and creature being eliminated
        iii. Distinction between animals and humans being eliminated
    c. Politics—totalitarian state seeks to eliminate distinction between itself and its citizenry
    d. Religion
        i. Hindu notion of *advaita* proposed as the spiritual way forward
        ii. Collapse of distinction between God and us
        iii. Yoga and Buddhist mindfulness now promoted in some schools
    e. Theology
        i. Progressive Christianity without any creeds, dogmas, or notion of unique Scripture
        ii. The next stage of Christianity as interfaith
    f. Eschatology—losing distinction between heaven and hell
    g. Gender—gender distinctions continually attacked

STUDY QUESTIONS

1. There is a growing attempt to redefine human civilization based on the notion that man is god.
    a. True
    b. False

2. Melanie Phillips stated that ________ is the battering ram against the fundamental tenets of Western culture, in order to destroy it and replace it with a new type of society altogether.
   a. Sexuality
   b. Spirituality
   c. Education
   d. Equality

3. Pagan thinking even seeks to try to eliminate the distinction between true and false.
   a. True
   b. False

4. Pitirim Sorokin, an escapee from Stalin's Soviet Union, stated that the first essential mark of civilization requires that ________.
   a. Families attend church
   b. Men take responsibility for their offspring
   c. Governments care for the poor
   d. A system of justice be established

5. The totalitarian state seeks to obliterate the distinction between itself and its citizenry.
   a. True
   b. False

BIBLE STUDY AND DISCUSSION QUESTIONS

1. Many today argue that the Christian notion of hell needs to be discarded, and that a loving God would not damn anyone. Explain how this line of reasoning is influenced by oneist ways of thinking.

2. Dr. Jones explains that it is not only toleration of non-Christian sexuality that is demanded, but also silence from the opposition. When should Christians voice their opinions in this matter, and how should they do it?

3. If the educational system is promulgating an essentially pagan worldview, how can Christian churches and families best counteract such teaching?

4. If paganism seeks to eliminate oppositions, including the distinction between right and wrong, how can there be any sense of justice? Contrast this pagan impulse with the Christian view of justice.

9

Unbiblical Responses

MESSAGE INTRODUCTION

In light of the cataclysmic cultural changes that have occurred during the recent past, Christians have responded in a number of ways. While some have sought to separate themselves completely from culture, others have attempted to make the Christian faith and worldview less objectionable by conforming it to the tastes of modern culture. In this lecture, we will see some ways that Christians have failed to maintain the distinctively Christian worldview, and why Christians cannot compromise on Christian worldview distinctives. Compromising the Christian worldview leads to compromising the gospel itself.

SCRIPTURE READINGS

1 John 2:15; Ephesians 2:1–10

TEACHING OBJECTIVES

1. To make clear why Christians cannot conform to the present culture
2. To show the ways in which Christians are intimidated to conform to the culture
3. To explore the results of a Christianity that has compromised with culture

QUOTATION

Be not conformed to this world. But what is conformity to the world? The opposite of conformity to Jesus: for Jesus and the world stand directly opposed to each other. The world crucified Him. He and His disciples are not of the world. The spirit of this world cannot receive the Spirit of God, for it sees Him not and knows Him not.

And what is the spirit of this world? The spirit of this world is the disposition that animates mankind in their natural condition, where the Spirit of God has not yet renewed them. The spirit of this world comes from the Evil One, who is the prince of this world, and has dominion over all that are not renewed by the Spirit of God.

—Andrew Murray

LECTURE OUTLINE

1. Christians should not conform to the culture.
    a. Studying the culture and making Christianity palatable to it is sociology rather than theology.
    b. The gospel is a message that comes from outside a culture and challenges it.
    c. Christians must reject the ideology of modern culture and its leaders while exhibiting love for sinners.
    d. Modern culture follows Satan and his lie.
    e. There is a radical difference between pagan oneism and Christian twoism, and they cannot be joined.

2. Christians are intimidated to conform to culture.
    a. Fear is one of the primary reasons to conform.
    b. Christians are tempted to modify their message to win cultural approval.
    c. Anti-Christian culture ends up determining what constitutes the acceptable Christian message.
        i. This is seen in the mainline denominations, which are loved by the culture.
        ii. Former evangelical Brian McLaren synthesizes Buddhist thought with Christianity.
        iii. Culturally acceptable views of sexuality are invading the church, and gender distinctions are being eliminated.
    d. Many seek a version of Christianity that is divorced from any creed or dogma.
        i. This leads to a rejection of the mind.
        ii. God needs to be experienced rather than understood.
        iii. This thinking is deeply influenced by Jung's work.

STUDY QUESTIONS

1. Carl Jung argued that the Christ symbol lacked wholeness, and that this wholeness is to be found in the reconciliation of the opposites of good and evil.
    a. True
    b. False

2. Studying the culture and modifying the Christian message to make it more acceptable is an example of ________ rather than theology.
    a. Paganism
    b. Sociology
    c. Anthropology
    d. Gnosticism

3. Fear has not been a major factor for Christians to conform their message to the surrounding culture.
    a. True
    b. False

4. Carl Jung thought that ________ ________ would create an irresistible mass movement that would undermine two thousand years of Christianity.
   a. Sexual freedom
   b. Spiritual renewal
   c. Pagan theology
   d. Environmental movements

5. Those who advocate a religionless Christianity, devoid of any creed or dogma, tend to deemphasize the use of the mind in their spirituality.
   a. True
   b. False

BIBLE STUDY AND DISCUSSION QUESTIONS

1. Fear is a major reason for Christians to modify their message in order to make it more acceptable to the culture. Read 2 Timothy 1:3–7 and give some examples of why Christians can be bold in standing for the truth.

2. Have you ever been tempted to articulate an aspect of the Christian faith and worldview in a more culturally acceptable way? What motivated this?

3. Disagreeing with modern culture's spirituality can lead to hostility and rejection. How can Christians show genuine love in their presentation of the gospel while at the same time refusing to compromise their beliefs?

4. The impulse to eliminate gender distinctions has even crept into some evangelical churches. Explain how this is part of a wider pagan worldview, and why it is wrong.

10

Articulating a Biblical Worldview

MESSAGE INTRODUCTION

In the previous lesson, we looked at ways in which Christians should not react to the hostility of modern culture. In this lesson, we will see what Christians should do. They must first understand the opposition's worldview (a major goal of this series), and then they must clearly affirm the superiority of the Christian worldview with its twoist view of reality.

SCRIPTURE READINGS

1 Peter 3:13–17; Colossians 4:6

TEACHING OBJECTIVES

1. To show how Christians must respond to the pagan worldview of modern culture
2. To explain the oneist and twoist views of humanity
3. To point out the fundamental areas where individuals can either worship the Creator or the creation

QUOTATION

There are several wrong views respecting the seat of religion in man. Some think of religion primarily as a sort of knowledge, and locate it in the intellect. Others regard it as a kind of immediate feeling of God, and find its seat in the feelings. And still others hold that it consists most of all in moral activity, and refer it to the will. However, all these views are one-sided and contrary to Scripture, which teaches us that religion is a matter of the heart. In Scripture the heart is the central organ of the soul. Out of it are all the issues of life, thoughts, feelings, and desires, Prov. 4:28. Religion involves the whole man, his intellectual, his emotional, and his moral life. This is the only view that does justice to the nature of religion.

—Louis Berkhof

LECTURE OUTLINE

1. There are two things Christians must do in response to the pagan worldview of modern culture.
    a. They must have a clear understanding of the opposition.
    b. They must have a clear understanding of twoism and they must publicly affirm it.
2. Twoism is the only system that cannot be dominated by oneism.
    a. Oneist religions reject Christian twoism.
    b. Christians must speak and live the twoist worldview with courage, coherence, and love.
    c. The confrontation is not simply between thinkers, but between passionate worshipers.
3. The biblical faith is unique.
    a. It was unique in the ancient world and continues to be unique today.
    b. The same conflict between believers and unbelievers has continued throughout history.
    c. For 1700 years, the Christian West has largely honored the principle of twoism.
4. The real struggle in our time is the question of identity for humanity.
    a. Twoism affirms the distinction between the Creator and humanity, and within humanity between male and female.
    b. Oneism rejects the distinction between man and God, and between male and female.
    c. For Christians, the answer regarding who we are comes not from within, but from outside ourselves, through the revelation of God.
        i. Humans can acknowledge that revelation and worship the Creator.
        ii. Humans can reject that revelation and worship the creation.
    d. Christians have a basis for morality in a personal God, but pagans do not.
5. In Romans 1, Paul shows three fundamental areas where humans can either worship the Creator or the creation.
    a. Theology
        i. One can recognize God as Creator of heaven and earth, and thus separate from them.
        ii. One can choose nature as divine.
    b. Spirituality
        i. One can worship God and have no others before Him.
        ii. One can worship nature and the things therein.
    c. Sexuality
        i. One can acknowledge the differences between the two sexes.
        ii. One can exchange their natural functions with those that are contrary to nature.
6. Christians cannot be silent on the reality of sin.

STUDY QUESTIONS

1. The only system that oneism cannot dominate is twoism.
   a. True
   b. False

2. Dr. Jones relies on ________ when contrasting the Christian and pagan views of God.
   a. Romans 2
   b. Galatians 1
   c. Romans 1
   d. Hebrews 2

3. If people do not understand the relationship of "creation" and "the fall," they will never understand redemption.
   a. True
   b. False

4. Paul points out three fundamental areas where one can serve either the Creator or the creation. These are spirituality, sexuality, and ________.
   a. Theology
   b. Anthropology
   c. Psychology
   d. Art

5. The real struggle of the modern age is the identity of humanity.
   a. True
   b. False

BIBLE STUDY AND DISCUSSION QUESTIONS

1. Why is it necessary that a Christian have a clear understanding of his or her opponent's worldview?

2. Dr. Jones notes that the confrontation between oneism and twoism is not simply between thinkers, but between passionate worshipers. How does a recognition of this fact inform disagreements between the differing views?

3. Paganism has neither a personal God nor an ethical universe. How can you use these facts to challenge someone who holds a pagan viewpoint?

4. Explain the different views of humanity espoused by oneism and twoism.

11

Living in Holiness

MESSAGE INTRODUCTION

When surrounded by a culture that indulges itself in much sexual perversion, how should Christians respond? In his letter to the Romans, the Apostle Paul addresses a context similar to the one believers face today. He argued that Christians must live holy lives, which not only pleases God, but also provides an example of godliness for the wider world. In this lecture, Dr. Jones explores what it means to live in holiness, and what that looks like in our many contexts.

SCRIPTURE READINGS

Romans 12:1; 1 Corinthians 6:20

TEACHING OBJECTIVES

1. To exhort Christians to holy living
2. To show why Christians should live in holiness
3. To explore how Christians can live holy lives

QUOTATION

No one will travel so badly as not daily to make some degree of progress. This, therefore, let us never cease to do, that we may daily advance in the way of the Lord; and let us not despair because of the slender measure of success. How little soever the success may correspond with our wish, our labour is not lost when today is better than yesterday, provided with true singleness of mind we keep our aim, and aspire to the goal, not speaking flattering things to ourselves, nor indulging our vices, but making it our constant endeavour to become better, until we attain to goodness itself. If during the whole course of our life we seek and follow, we shall at length attain it, when relieved from the infirmity of flesh we are admitted to full fellowship with God.

—John Calvin

LECTURE OUTLINE

1. In chapter 12 of Romans, Paul exhorts believers to bodily holiness and to thinking with transformed minds.
    a. The Roman world indulged in much sexual perversion.
    b. Christians today live in a similar context, and Paul's words carry the same demand for holiness today.
    c. Paul is not advocating moralism but our response to undeserved mercy.

2. Reasons for living with holy bodies
    a. Our body language must agree with our speech in public—no one likes a hypocrite.
    b. Our bodies are visible witnesses to God the Creator.
    c. Christianity is not Gnosticism, which rejects the body.
        i. Christians must beware of incipient Gnosticism in the church which commits to a spiritual agenda while allowing sexual freedom.
        ii. The biblical view is committed to the spiritual and the physical.
        iii. The Christian's body will be saved and raised.

3. Christians are holy—they have been set apart.

4. The answer to how to live is submission.
    a. Wives submit to their husbands.
    b. Husbands sacrifice their lives for their wives.

5. God is glorified by a holy life.

6. Holiness is corporate.
    a. The Bible speaks of the holiness of Christ's body, the church.
    b. The church is called a "holy priesthood."
    c. Christ's goal for the church is that she would be holy and without blemish.
    d. Our lives are to be self-sacrificial for one another, following Christ's example.

7. Holiness is a noble calling.

STUDY QUESTIONS

1. Christians are supposed to live holy lives in order to prove they're better than everyone else.
    a. True
    b. False

2. The primary meaning of holiness is ________.
    a. Being set apart
    b. Living a moral life
    c. Thinking with discernment
    d. Worshiping with reverence

3. Because a person's soul is more important than his body, what he does with his body is of less importance.
    a. True
    b. False

4. The Greek term *cosmos* means ________ in English.
    a. Matter
    b. The world
    c. The ordered universe
    d. The earth as opposed to the sky

5. There are certain Christians today who have a unique call to holiness.
    a. True
    b. False

BIBLE STUDY AND DISCUSSION QUESTIONS

1. How does the Islamic view of gender distinctions demonstrate that it is not a consistently twoist religion?

2. Explain the relationship between the distinctions God has placed in the universe and the biblical view of submission. How should this lead to individual bodily holiness?

3. What are the primary reasons that Christians should strive to live holy lives?

4. How can you encourage a fellow believer to holy living when he does not feel his occupation or time has great significance in God's plan?

12

Thinking with a Discerning Mind

MESSAGE INTRODUCTION

Unbelieving thought is based on a worldview that is completely antithetical to the Christian faith. The previous lessons have sought to articulate some of the core beliefs of this pagan worldview, and this lecture aims to look specifically at pagan, oneist thinking, and to contrast it with Christian twoism.

SCRIPTURE READINGS

Romans 12:2; 2 Timothy 4:3

TEACHING OBJECTIVES

1. To demonstrate the need for Christians to have a transformed, discerning mind
2. To show the difference between a discerning and undiscerning mind
3. To explain how twoism affects one's thinking in many different ways

QUOTATION

Mingled vanity and pride appear in this, that when miserable men do seek after God, instead of ascending higher than themselves as they ought to do, they measure him by their own carnal stupidity, and, neglecting solid inquiry, fly off to indulge their curiosity in vain speculation. Hence, they do not conceive of him in the character in which he is manifested, but imagine him to be whatever their own rashness has devised. This abyss standing open, they cannot move one footstep without rushing headlong to destruction. With such an idea of God, nothing which they may attempt to offer in the way of worship or obedience can have any value in his sight, because it is not him they worship, but, instead of him, the dream and figment of their own heart.

—John Calvin

LECTURE OUTLINE

1. Christians need a transformed mind.
    a. The sinful mind constructs itself on the basis of the lie that creation is divine.
    b. Christians must clearly discern the difference between truth and lie.

2. There are two kinds of minds.
    a. The undiscerning mind
        i. Makes nature god and serves it
        ii. Suppresses the truth
        iii. Seeks a synthesis that joins opposites
        iv. Builds a oneist worldview
    b. The discerning mind
        i. Must be a transformed mind due to inherent sin
        ii. Acknowledges God as Creator and serves Him
        iii. Sees antithesis between truth and falsehood
        iv. Recognizes a twoist worldview
    c. These two kinds of mind must answer the basic question, "Does the world create itself, or does a Creator?"

3. We live in a world committed to a oneist vision.

4. The transformed mind must learn how to think about the world in light of the fundamental truth that God is separate from us.

5. Twoism affects our thinking in numerous ways.
    a. Theology
        i. Acknowledges Creator/creature distinction
        ii. God is sovereign and transcendent.
        iii. As creatures we submit to God and serve Him. Therein we find our dignity.
        iv. People cannot know who they are without knowing who God is.
    b. Meaning
        i. Oneism is condemned to human circular reasoning.
        ii. Twoism relies on outside revelation from God.
        iii. History has a meaningful beginning and end.
    c. Morality
        i. Twoism affirms that there is right and wrong.
        ii. Good and evil are distinct and must not be joined.
    d. Redemption
        i. It is not self-salvation, but the act of a Creator for helpless sinners.
        ii. It brings freedom from guilt, which cannot come from within.
    e. Spirituality
        i. Prayer is not reflection, but communion with the Creator.
        ii. Praise can only be for oneself in oneism. It is praise of the other in twoism.

6. The incarnation solves the problem of God and humanity without destroying twoism.

7. Christians are on the side of truth, which is God's side.

STUDY QUESTIONS

1. The undiscerning mind makes nature god, serves the creation, and builds a worldview of oneism, which will eventually collapse because it is not based on the truth.
    a. True
    b. False
2. Dr. Jones notes that ________ is only possible within a twoist worldview.
    a. Giving
    b. Praise
    c. Spirituality
    d. Sexuality
3. The only question one can fundamentally ask about origins is, "Does the world create itself, or does a Creator make it?"
    a. True
    b. False
4. All of the following except ________ apply to the union of the divine and human natures of the Son of God in His incarnation.
    a. Perfectly mixed
    b. Unchanging
    c. Undivided
    d. Inseparable
5. When people reject God as Creator, they cannot properly understand who they are as humans.
    a. True
    b. False

BIBLE STUDY AND DISCUSSION QUESTIONS

1. Explain how only twoism allows for genuine salvation.

2. What are some ways that you could convince someone who doesn't believe in right and wrong that their position is untenable?

3. Explain how the Christian faith, with its uniquely twoist worldview, is the only way that one can experience relief of guilt.

4. How does the incarnation, as the union of God and man, preserve twoism?